The Youth Marketing Academy Presents

Fans: from Liked to Loved

by
Graham Brown
and
Ghani Kunto

Copyright: mobileYouth
Published: 1st Oct 2012 Publisher: mobileYouth

The right of Graham Brown and Ghani Kunto to be identified as authors of this Work has been asserted in accordance with sections 77 and 78 of the Copyright, Designs and Patents Act 1988. All rights reserved. No part of this publication may be reproduced, stored in retrieval system, copied in any form or by any means, electronic, mechanical, photocopying, recording or otherwise transmitted without written permission from the publisher. You must not circulate this book in any format.

www.YouthMarketingAcademy.com

TABLE OF CONTENTS

THE YOUTH MARKETING ACADEMY'S 10 KEY RULES OF FANS IN 200 WORDS...

INTRODUCTION 1
    HALO vs MINECRAFT: REVOLUTION IN SHELF-SPACE
    FANS > AGENCIES

THE CHANGE 9
    THE NEW COOL
    THE LONG TAIL OF PASSION
    THE INTEREST ECONOMY: A LOVE STORY
    WASIT GOBLOG: HERE COMES THE INTERNET

WHY ARE FANS IMPORTANT? 25
    LIKED vs LOVED
    AWARENESS MEANS NOTHING
    FANS (NOT AD AGENCIES) NOW DETERMINE YOUR CONTEXT
    LEGO FANS: THE POWER OF FANS
    VS THE FANS: WIKIPEDIA
    EVERYONE HAS FANS: NOODLES

WHO ARE THEY? 39
    FAUX-FANS
    FANS vs EARLY ADOPTERS: TREVOR MORAN

FANS: TRUE BRAND CUSTODIANS
WHAT DO THEY WANT?..................................47
MONSTER ARMY: ASHTON'S STORY
DOTHRAKI: THE IMPORTANCE OF SIGNALLING COSTS
HOW DO WE GIVE IT TO THEM? 59
GANGNAM STYLE: OBSCURITY
SCUMBAG STEVE: WHY YOU CAN'T OWN YOUR OWN MEME
THE PEOPLE vs GEORGE LUCAS
FROM STAR WARS TO HARRY POTTER: INTERNET FANDOMS AND FAN-FICTION
A HOME FOR FANS
WHEN FAN ENGAGEMENT GOES WRONG
DON'T TREAT FANS LIKE KIDS AT THE MUSEUM
AUTHORS 77
THE YOUTH MARKETING ACADEMY.........79

THE YOUTH MARKETING ACADEMY'S 10 KEY RULES OF FANS

1. Fans > agencies
2. Every brand has Fans, even yours
3. If you don't know who your Fans are you have only customers
4. If customers like you, be afraid, be very afraid
5. Awareness means nothing. When was the last time you bought a Cadillac?
6. The Interest Economy is the Long Tail of identity
7. There is no "official" brand story anymore
8. You can't compete with Fans
9. Rather than ask "how do we engage Fans?" we need to be asking "how do we break down the walls that prevent Fans from engaging us?"
10. Find your fans, the rest is mere detail

IN 200 WORDS...

Focus on the 10% who already love your product.

Forget about the 90% who need to be sold. Sell only to the sold. The 90% aren't listening to you anyway. Youth don't wake up thinking about your brand anymore. Get over it. The 90% listens only to the 10%. Fans are the influencers. What Fans say about your product is far more important than what your creative agency says. And here's where it gets difficult. Fans own the brand. When your brand manager goes to sleep, Fans stay up to the early hours, building, creating and sharing. Fans are passionate. They *love* the brand. There is no official "brand story" anymore, just a plethora of parallel narratives told by Fans. Each, a personal take on what the brand does for them. Fans are changing everything we know about marketing; brand management, the "Big Idea" and creative advertising are all being made redundant.

Without Fans, your brand just has customers. But to win the Fans, your role is to curate rather than create. Forget about "having a conversation" with them. They're not interested in you or your brand. They are only interested in how you will connect them with each other.

INTRODUCTION

HALO vs MINECRAFT: REVOLUTION IN SHELF-SPACE

There is a quiet revolution under way.

On the one hand, the usual suspects: Lady Gaga, X-Men and Halo Reach. Like Gaga and X-Men, the game Halo Reach is a big hitter; it cost $60m to produce and a further $40m to secure distribution, PR and marketing. Sales passed $300m which means the publishers (now Microsoft by virtue of their subsidiary 343Industries) netted a cool $200m. These are tried and tested franchises that are low risk and can deliver.

On the other, the anomalies - video games like Minecraft. Minecraft netted significantly less than Halo Reach ($100m a year) but consider those figures in the context of sustainability and ROI. In terms of sustainability, Minecraft has a legacy that will continue to yield returns year in year out until either the company or the fans desert the platform. It's a system that requires minimal marketing and ongoing product development (the Fans take care of all of that). And, it's a system that cost less than $100k to set up (the creator's estimated salary for 1 year of development).

So, compare the ROI. In the world of the Big Idea, the Big Hit and an attitude of "Go Big or Go Home," our world is governed by the concept of "mental shelf space." There can only be one item at the top of the retailer's best seller chart. There are only a select few titles that receive the attention of the full window displays, in-store concessions and staff promotions. When shelf-space is limited, your marketing aim is to secure the largest possible return that's why you'd pick a Lady Gaga over a small niche genre artist or Reach over a less well known title. Small hits barely cover the cost of development and marketing. Small hits go home.

The "fat head" of entertainment will be around for a long time yet. When Microsoft can make $200m by milking a successful franchise it will continue to attract investment. $200m doesn't disappear overnight. Hasbro releases a movie based on Battleship and develops another based on Monopoly. X-Men iterations will continue to run and we, the public, will continue to go and line up and watch them even though they are welcomed by lukewarm reviews.

But now there are options. We don't need to run our business like McDonald's anymore. We don't need to be big by dominating our sector through economies of scale. In the McBusiness model, Halo Reach yielded a return of 3:1. Compare these returns with Minecraft where returns pass 1,000:1 and continue to generate dividends even when Halo Reach has been confined to the discount bin at the retailers.

It's a revolution that is redefining content. Where the "shelf-space" was once the recommendation of a DJ, a radio station playlist or a magazine interview, musical genres and tastes have exploded in line with a parallel growth in media outlets. Google "Rolling in the Deep" by big-hitter Adele and you'll also find hundreds of covers varying from solo acoustic renditions to Mike Posner remixes. Music discovery is no longer limited to mental shelf-space but now carried by countless armies of Fans who willingly share their findings. Wannabe artists no longer need labels for distribution and promotion, the braver bands now turn to services like Bandcamp where they can manage and control their own destiny straight out of the box. Nor do they need MTV rotation to hit the big time, they can get that from cameos and features on startups channels like SBTV - run originally out the back of a bedroom - have over 150,000 subscribers and nearly 100 million views.

When Chris Anderson wrote "The Long Tail" he challenged us to rethink long held notions of economics. We started reassessing the whole idea of the "big hit" and the "top 10." The missing link in this story is, however, the people that make the Long Tail possible. When we're offered a Long Tail of options in every category imaginable - from music to lifestyle - our notions of behavior and identity will also change. This "Interest Economy" will unite people based on passion not geography. We've long talked up the digital revolution as an industry waxing lyrical about new frontiers offered by mobile and Facebook but this isn't a technology story, it's a human one. It's a story about Fans.

The Long Tail increasingly provides an equally attractive option but it's not simply a case of switching it on - embracing the Long Tail is not a question of strategy but of mindset. Minecraft embraced Fans from day one, involving them in innovation of texture packs, ongoing testing and building Minecon events to house their dialogue.

The promise of the Interest Economy is a win-win. Minecraft is played across 90 countries and it doesn't need to hire expensive agencies or customer service in each country to cover localization or language issues. The Interest Economy has little respect for borders be they linguistic, ethnic or racial. Minecraft players can be

German, Japanese or Brazilian and they'll still play on equal terms. The promise for the customer is of connection - a platform to meet these likeminds outside of the confines of the mainstream. For the company, the promise is felt on the bottom line. Minecraft doesn't deal with the "we're different here" attitude of organizational fiefdoms or agency heads that convince brands to impart their marketing budgets on the basis of secret local insights. Lego doesn't manufacture special Indian bricks for its customers in India. The Interest Economy defies traditional approaches to segmentation.

In the Minecraft model, Fans volunteer to service each other, removing expensive, centralized call centers. Could Fans turn customer service from being a "cost center" in the business to its best marketing strategy? Fan marketing is word of mouth through people just like you. Innovation is real time by the users for the users. What companies need to do isn't to engage an agency in creating a social business campaign or to design strategy. Companies simply need to let go.

Letting go means less management, more facilitation. It means curation rather than control and that is the real challenge. The challenge isn't a question of finding the right business model to make it work but the right people whose mindset is open to change and that means embracing Fans.

Embracing Fans means opening the door to a brave new world of The Interest Economy in its many guises - from Minecraft to Hipsters to, dare I say it, Bronies. Fans go to work while your creative agency sleeps. Fans are the key to 1,000x returns on marketing. Fans are to traditional segmentation what the Long Tail is to shelf space and they are redefining the rules of marketing whether you like it or not.

FANS > AGENCIES

I recently read about BlackBerry's attempts to undermine an Apple product launch by a guerrilla marketing campaign that employed a "busload of paid activists" to heckle the store. There are perhaps too many things wrong with this approach to go into detail here, suffice to say that one factor underpins all of them - the creative agency.

Dante once wrote "there are a thousand people striking at the branches of evil for everyone striking at the root." In marketing terms, this isn't about creating a more engaging campaign, a better conversation with customers or a more viral video. It's about erasing the ad agency from the equation. Smart ad agencies will know this and will go to work redefining their role in this set up. Dumb ones will tell you how many awards they won for their last campaign.

65% of youth bought their handset because of what their *peers* not what the *creative agency* said. If you want one statistic to convince your coworkers that the Fan revolution is real, then use this one.

To see how this revolution is impacting our daily lives look at how Fans are already making significant inroads into the behaviors that count. No creative agency was ever successful in convincing you to send a text message, use Facebook or even read this document on Kindle. The most widely used services - Facebook, Instagram, Kik, WhatsApp, BBM and SMS have reached mass market adoption as a result of Fans spreading the technology from student to student not through creative agencies. If creative agencies were effective, why don't they advertise themselves?

When I posed this question to an industry adversary from a well known ad agency he replied, "we don't need to advertise because we build our business through word of mouth and recommendation." Enough said.

If you want to engage the youth market, you'd be better off starting with Fans. Of course, this approach won't win you any *fans* with your agency but it's not worth wasting your energies on those that don't get it. Focus on the 10% who do and work on them to convert the 90%. Not only is this a good maxim to guide your internal sell, it's also the basis of youth marketing.

A word of advice: engaging the 10% isn't easy. You can't throw a large marketing budget at it. You can't employ an award winning agency. You can't trade off having a "cool youth brand." You have to do the work. There you go, it's that simple (and difficult). You've got to get out there, organize the events, organize the hackathons, be part of that community and that's a step too far for the guy who spent his whole career trying to get a bigger office not more time on the street. I know what some people may think when they hear that. "I didn't do my MBA to go out there and talk to kids." Well, when Tony Hsieh (CEO) of Zappos is in the office, he's on the phone talking to customers. These customers become Fans. That 10% gave Zappos a core of vocal supporters. Hsieh sold his company to Amazon for $928 million. CEOs need to lead by example.

Fans tell each other about the Zappos story. Every brand has Fans, even companies who are in denial, like Nokia. The problem is that handset companies, for example, speak to their ad agencies and get convinced that their Fans could be just like those crazy Apple Fans who camp outside the retail stores waiting for the latest iPhone. They're told that if they want to compete with Apple, they've got to "outcool" them. Bad advice.

If you want to compete with Apple, you've got to do like Apple and be true to your core DNA. Nokia Fans and Apple Fans are distinct, it's just that Apple is the only brand of the two that is actively supporting its Fans. Nokia has a problem accepting that its fans love the indestructible 3300. There are far more odes and homages on YouTube and meme websites to the vintage 3300 than the Nokia Lumia but rather than accept this truth, the creative agency instead builds castles in the sky by prodding their real Fans to wax lyrical about the Lumia and MS OS than what they really love.

Fans of sushi restaurants aren't fans of McDonalds so why should McDonald's try and grab the cooler crowd? McDonald's is far more profitable than any sushi restaurant in the world so who has the better business model?

Find your fans, the rest is mere detail. Every brand has fans, though few have activate them.

THE CHANGE

THE NEW COOL

Today, it's hard to sell cool, because nobody knows what that is anymore.

Driven by fan discussions online, a show that one television network deemed "made TV too gay" actually became a top hit. The Gleeks, as the Glee fans call themselves, proudly show their love for the show. Make a nerdy TV show like Glee, Ugly Betty, or Big Bang Theory and you'll find a fan base. Make a geeky movie about comic book superheroes like Iron Man you'll find Fans of all ages. Nobody needs to hide their inner nerd anymore. This is the new sincerity of the Interest Economy, where guilty pleasures are just pleasures.

Being a nerd is cool now. But being cool is also still cool. Perhaps the term "nerd" is simply a term coined by mainstream media to control, corral and terrorize a vastly diversified and unique group of individuals into believing in a myth of the mainstream.

When we were kids we were told to "be ourselves" but it was a difficult advice to action. It was too hard to just be ourselves. "Being myself" often meant "being by myself" and nobody wanted that especially young people. If you loved comics, like my co-author, Ghani, you'd have to wear shades and a baseball cap when you went to to your local comic store. You avoided eye contact with other customers. Back at school you were into football just like the other jocks because being part of the group is more important than being ourselves. Most youth would rather go on an unhealthy diet to look like the models they saw in that cool advert where it seemed like everybody had friends. Some young people took the other route, and thought they could get friends if they emulated the romanticized image of bad boys who sat in the back of the class.

Today, while many young people are still trying to fit themselves into the traditional ideals about cool many more are discovering and defining what cool is for themselves. Cool is just a Google search away.

Today, youth can be themselves without being *by themselves*. The Interest Economy is a growing diaspora of Fans united not by geographical proximity - as was the haphazard zip code lottery of friendships in the pre-internet era - but by passions. If youth can now define their own cool, advertising no longer plays a central role in their story. The Pepsi Generation is over.

Storytelling - the art of the advertiser - has now become the prerogative of the customer. In particular, the young customer. More specifically the young Fan. It's here in these self-defined stories about what brands are and are *not* that youth shape the fortunes of billion dollar companies. Young black South African females redefine the story of an executive messaging tool to create one of the country's most identifiable brands - BlackBerry. Millions spent on ad agencies trying to make Nokia cool fail to impress a whole new generation of customers for whom the brand means very little.

In the era of Earned Media the story isn't written by the brand manager or ad agency but by the customer and it's this change in mindset that forms the fundamental prerequisite of getting strategy right. You can't generate Earned Media if you're out there with a bullhorn shouting your story. You have to let the Fans tell the story.

We no longer live in era of mainstream and "alternative"; now everything is alternative.

THE LONG TAIL OF PASSION

"Magical things can happen when you enthusiastically open your mouth on the internet." wrote Kevin Zelnio on his blog covering Deep Sea News.

Deep Sea News isn't going to make it to the mainstream anyday but to say it's not important is to misunderstand the role of today's Interest Economy. Zelnio attended a Science Online Conference in 2011 and was frustrated that his passions were constantly challenged by mainstream orthodoxy. He felt compelled to post his feelings online coupled with the hashtag "#iamascientist".

Zelnio's raw sentiment captured the feelings of the scientific diaspora. But these were not prodigious Einsteins or socially awkward lab rats. These scientists were everybody from students who were once homeless as teens, to those who became interested in medicine when a friend got sick.

In the Tumblr blog "This is what a scientist looks like http://lookslikescience.tumblr.com/" we are challenged to review our stereotypes about who scientists really are. Below a picture of a young female benchpressing 100lb weights lies the caption "I am an entomologist. Crossfit keeps me in shape for chasing bugs."

The Loudspeaker needs stereotypes because a single narrative cannot entertain the nebulous. In the world of the Loudspeaker there is only the mainstream and the nerds, no prizes for guessing where scientists would be found. When we open the box on the Interest Economy our models of communication break down - how can one narrative work for this complex fabric of different backgrounds, lifestyles and attitudes? Why do Brian Cox and Doctor Who attract an inordinate amount of female Fans when their subject areas are traditionally male?

When we are forced to discard stereotypes we are also forced to entertain every story on its own unique terms, replete with fears, hopes and passions. In the Loudspeaker model, the Interest Economy is a threat - suppressed by terms like "nerd" and "geek" - but our future lies in these digitally connected diasporas. The Loudspeaker Era is a bygone era, now replaced by the Telephone Era. Today it's about allowing fans to tell their own story and accepting that their version of events, brands and history may be different to ours. A Fan's interpretation of a brand may not conform with the brand template but it doesn't become any less valid.

Zelnio's story, that of a scientist frustrated by mainstream orthodoxy, is the story of every Fan on this planet. Whether she is a self-confessed comic geek, weightlifter or librarian, the mainstream represents a constant compromise of interests. The mainstream is liked by all and loved by none. That's why the Fans that have passions don't fit into the mainstream model. We see them as a threat. But, if we are to realize that we can work with this energy, we open the door the all the upside of the Interest

Economy. We need to harness rather than contain their passions and working with rather than against Fans.

Every fan has a story to tell. You may not have to like it but you have to be cool with it.

THE INTEREST ECONOMY: A LOVE STORY

"My boyfriend proposed to me on Minecraft," wrote Vegyangel on 13th October 2010 on YouTube.

She prefaced her video with a short personal story that provided context to her 2 minute video and then invited in the YouTube community to praise or shoot her down in flames.

Vegyangel's story forced many emotive responses from viewers, the first question being "What the heck is Minecraft?" and the second being, "Why on Earth did he propose to you on it?"

Most girls don't grow up dreaming of their boyfriend proposing to them on Minecraft. But that's exactly the point. This isn't about *most* girls. It's about one girl and what was meaningful to her. Let me first start by answering the first question. And no, I'm not a Minecraft user but I've discovered enough about it and interacted with users to gain an objective proposal of what it is.

Minecraft is an online game. "*Minecraft* is a game about placing blocks to build anything you can imagine," explains the company website. At first glance, Minecraft appears to be some form of throwback to the 8 bit days of games arcades that make Space Invaders look advanced. A square cartoon figure navigates a 3D world full of coarse, blocky landscapes that can be shaped, moved and destroyed by the player. Graphically, Minecraft is from the Stone Age but that's where its appeal lies.

The aim of the Minecraft game appears to be completely governed by mutual consensus - there is no official narrative. You simply turn up and build stuff. Some people play, get bored and leave. But for others, they gather into teams and create intricate reconstructions of the Taj Mahal, medieval Europe or New York City. Friends can explore worlds and build together without a predetermined script or set rule of play. Some, like Vegyangel, meet their soul mates working on a replica of the ancient Pyramids of Egypt or canals of Venice, while others simply hang out online with their real world friends drawing blueprints and discussing future projects.

Similar to Lego, the strength of Minecraft has been in its simplicity. In a world where blockbuster Xbox titles will cost $30m + and teams of programmers to develop, Minecraft was created by a single individual - Markus Persson or "Notch" as he is affectionately known - in his apartment. Now, before you dismiss Minecraft as one of the many weird and wonderful fantasy worlds on the internet consider a few of the headline figures. Minecraft makes $100m a year with a minimal development and marketing budget, a team of 6 full time programmers and a budget that struggles to reach into the millions. By 2012, one year after the paid version of Minecraft went public, there were 5 million paying customers and 1 million app downloads on the iTunes store. Note: *paid*. You can play the free version or you can voluntarily pay for a more advanced one.

Minecraft doesn't advertise - their Fans do everything for them. Search the countless community sites set up as homages to crafties and their passions or videos created of their creations and you start to see a fascinating, yet unknown world emerge:

* Number of YouTube results for search on "Minecraft": 2.6 million
* Highest ranking Minecraft related video: "Revenge" - A Minecraft Parody of Usher's DJ Got Us Fallin' in Love (Crafted using Minecraft Blocks) (23 million views)

"Minecraft now has 20 million registered users," announced Markus Persson on 16th January 2012, "At 70 kg each, that's 25% of the weight of the Great Pyramid of Giza."

Persson's dry Scandinavian humor would be lost on most. He's a "nerd" by his own confessions, claiming to have once made a "turing complete hexagon based cellular automata thingie" (??).

Which brings us to the second question, "Why on Earth did he propose to you on it?"

Now, having been a computing graduate at University in the 90s I quickly discovered that IT and girls did not mix. Computing was the domain of kids in sweaty Red Dwarf t-shirts, crowding round Ved terminals playing an online text form of Dungeons and Dragons 24 hours a day. The only time they were forced out into the "real" world was when a bearded sysadmin in slippers entered the computer labs and informed them the mainframe was being rebooted - a process that would (in those days) take hours rather than minutes. Computers weren't conducive to finding girls.

My prejudices are still rife today in how the YouTube community reacted to Vegyangel's proposal post:

"Nerds!!!!!!"

"My god, lamest proposal ever."

"Please marry him and then we can sterilise the pair or you and remove two mintards from the gene pool. Minecraft, a game so dumb you need learning difficulties to appreciate it."

"seriously? thats what you call a proposal?! how about take me for a nice meal, for once, and getting down on one knee with an actual ring, you cheap docuhe [sic] *?!?"*

The Loudspeaker survives by protecting itself.

The infallibility of Loudspeaker marketing cannot tolerate multiple narratives meaning those who don't subscribe to the cultural hegemony are a threat. Words like "cool" and "nerd" are used not by force but through consensus and with the help of the Pepsi Generation, we believe and propagate the imagery that terrorizes those outside the mainstream. Models that rely on a single narrative of what is "normal" become suspicious of other narratives labeling them as "subcultures," "alternative" perhaps even dangerous. We're scared of nerds at school - they're the kids that media leads us to believe pack pipe-bombs in their backpacks while they stare with faraway glazed expressions in class.

"Nerds" aren't the Pepsi Generation. These are kids who play Dungeons and Dragons, middle aged men who read comics, housewives playing FarmVille online, Minecraft dads with their sons or teenage girls into Korean Pop. But, then who's to decide now? Who controls what is "normal" or "mainstream" and what isn't? Perhaps these concepts are becoming increasingly irrelevant in marketing and the "Big Idea" of a homogenous narrative inappropriate to a growing number of people who have the tools to access a web of options and now want to decide things for themselves.

At a recent Ogilvy conference, the agency passed around flyers that encouraged their clients and employees to "ditch the nerds and see you at the bar." Ad agencies still have a problem with "nerds" not because they are too cool for these mere mortals but because the very existence of an "alternative" is, by definition, a threat to the mainstream. Most ad agencies are after all merely Proles for the Loudspeaker in all its monolithic boringness.

This is the modern Interest Economy that digital creates through unlimited shelf-space. No longer are we unified by geography but by passion. Across borders, growing numbers of people once confined to submission and compromise by the hegemony of mainstream advertising are now finding those with similar passions in differing countries, social strata or age groups. Now, you don't have to build model airplanes on your own - you can do it with others in China, Japan and Kenya. If you're into Vampires, the Roman Empire or even Star Wars there's someone out there waiting to build something with you. For many, it's a dream come true.

When we start to question our monolithic interpretation of normal we see a structure finely tuned to McBusiness not the digital age. Vegyangel shares her surprise in the Minecraft story, writing, "This was made the first week we both got Minecraft. He kept stopping to pick up flowers and wouldn't tell me why. This was in October 2010. We got married in August 2011."

Who decides what is an appropriate wedding proposal? Is the romantic guy the one that buys a ring that costs 3 months salary because he fears the reaction of his bride's parents? Is it the one who only buys his wife flowers on Valentine's day? Is it the one who, for fear of making a mistake, proposes in a way that wouldn't look out of place in a Hollywood movie? Surely, it's the one who cares nothing for criticism, prejudice and vindication to declare his undying love to another?

When Vegyangel delivered the answer to her beau on Minecraft the next day she did it by building an emphatic "YES" out of thousands of red blocks. In the Loudspeaker model, there is only one story and one interpretation of value. In the pre-digital era, it worked because most compromised or bottled up their passions and lack of tools to access meant you were stuck with the mainstream or forever living in the margins of the "alternative." Today, however, the very model is broken because by giving people mobile phones, Facebook and the internet, we've empowered millions to construct their own interpretations of context and value. Today, we are witnessing the fall of the model in the very advertising viewing and interaction habits of the next generation of consumers - today's teens and students.

With each day, the mainstream becomes smaller. Individuals flake off and find passions or interests that better suit them and the "nerds" eventually start to outweigh the rest. As commenters got stuck in with their nerd-bashing on the YouTube, a single commenter piped up seemingly oblivious to the public excoriation with a blunt question:

"What texture pack is this?"

Back in 2006 I remember employing a young German student who spoke openly about her passion for online role playing games like World of Warcraft. She spoke confidently, unashamed of stigmatization that plagued her forebears. Her confidence took me back. It's at that point I realized things had really changed. "Nerds" have found social validation in their own interests and are coming out of the closet, reclaiming the mainstream as their own. The Interest Economy is real and it's growing as we speak. We're all Nerds now.

The mainstream and, with it, the whole business of positioning, Big Ideas and brand management is dead. Embrace the Interest Economy.

WASIT GOBLOG: HERE COMES THE INTERNET

It was just another day in Twitterverse.

As usual, a collection of largely unconnected and often unknown topics dominated the global trending topics top 10. On that day, June 27th 2010 the top trending topic was #wasitgoblog.

People jumped in. Some rode the coattail of the trend, advertising their own content with links to articles like "7 Tips to Drive Traffic to Your Blog." Most however, were curious. What happened? Did it happen on Go Blog? What is Go Blog anyway?

Most of the tweets were not in English, tweets were in Indonesian. Asian Twitteratis were actually referring to the controversial call made by the referee in an England vs. Germany Soccer World Cup match. It was around 02:00 AM in Indonesia and most of those watching the game watched it in the comfort of their own homes. For a short moment in time, these total strangers voiced out a collective frustration. From a corner of the world that often receives little attention on the global media's stage came a voice that drowned out everything else on Twitter. Translated, #wasitgoblog means "stupid referee."

In a country of more than 300,000 islands, how else could an Indonesian fan of England's football team find so many others like her that they could overwhelm other things in Twitter? The internet is made of an infinite number of these small moments. Total strangers finding others who are passionate about some seemingly obscure thing. Fans of Call of Duty in Calgary, Canada play with a modded version of the game that was developed by another fan in Kandahar, Afghanistan. Fans of Japanese anime who like to dress up as their favorite characters find each other at regular cosplay festivals. Fans of Korean pop music in Mexico get together for karaoke parties.

This is the Interest Economy at work and the internet made it happen.

The internet became a place where all the things that didn't have space in the sound-bite-only traditional mass media found a voice. Things that seemed insignificant, even inane, to most, but very important to some now found a home. For many young people discovering and exploring their identity the Interest Economy offers an attractive alternative to the world of compromise and the Pepsi Generation approach offered by brand managers. You didn't have to be tall, blonde, perfectly good looking and dating the best looking guy in class when you were just 14. Just like previous generations youth wanted to be different but now they didn't have to be different alone.

For advertisers, the early internet held so much promise. Here was a new media that people were avidly paying attention to. Maybe this was the next television? Eyeballs translated to speculative growth and growth drove stock prices through the roof. The business model, it appeared, could be worked out later. Banner ads, pop-up ads, pop-under ads, the list goes on. Advertisers kept finding new ways to make sure plenty of eyeballs saw their advert.

Fast forward to post-dotcom-bust era, brands started to realize how much the internet is *not* like television. Yes, people consume this new media but the beauty of this media is that people can produce content too, and they are doing it to connect with others like them.

If John Lennon, Paul McCartney, George Harrison and Ringo Starr had only met today and made songs as legendary as The Beatles we know had, they still would not have been as successful as The Beatles were. They would still have the groupies, they would still rock their live shows but they could never reach 30 million album sales like The Beatles did with The White Album because you don't have to listen to the Beatles today to belong to your peer group - you have unlimited choice. I love "Paperback Writer," "A Day in the Life" and "Get Back." I'd perhaps even list them in my top 100 songs of all time but they aren't #1. And that is the point, The Beatles would have been in everybody's top 100, but not everybody's #1. The Beatles existed when there was just 1 music genre for their generation - Rock'n'roll.

You don't just have 1,000s of music genres to browse you could also be a Lego fan or be into World of Warcraft, My Little Pony, hang out on 4Chan, Hypebeast, Threadless or the millions of other community websites out there that house people just like you. In the 1960s you either liked the Fab 4 or you were "out."

In 2011, global recorded music sales lost a further $1.5bn. People just aren't buying albums anymore. No one can come near the record-breaking album sales numbers that artists used to get prior to the internet. Michael Jackson's *Thriller* was released in 1982 and sold 110 million copies. Even if you added up all the new album sales of 50 Cent, Justin Bieber, Coldplay and Beyonce in the last half of the decade, you won't come near those numbers.

From the troubadours of ancient Greek to singers who made it big via music videos and MTV to our current crop of household names, performance artists have always been the best storytellers. Their gift was the ability to enrapture their audience with charm and personality, along with on-stage performance. In today's world, while their names might be familiar across the globe, less and less people care enough to buy their albums because there are a million stories vying for the same number of eyeballs and ears. Now, musicians are just one type of storyteller among many. What chances do brands and advertisers have?

Today's storytellers (artists/brands/advertisers) might be better at telling their tales than their predecessors, but today's young people don't care. Young people today don't need or want a company telling them that they can become cooler if they're part of the some soda generation.

Soccer is popular in Indonesia, a country where Beckham and Messi roll off the tongue of young fans quicker than any of the homegrown talent. What makes the phenomenon interesting is that a large proportion of these fans are young girls. Young girls in a traditionally muslim country. It's a story few advertisers could have second guessed. When the cries of "wasit goblog" rippled around the Twitterverse, many of them were girls whose Twitter profiles featured the traditional hijab headscarf.

The internet changes how we market "cool" forever. No longer is "cool" even relevant because it represented a mainstream interpretation of how we should be. Today, the Interest Economy permits us to indulge our passions in communities that have found fertile soil on the internet. What matters today isn't the voice of aged DJs, magazine editorials and the images of the silver screen but the stories of the Fans, each and every one of them.

In the future, markets and marketing will be defined by passion and interest not by geography.

24

WHY ARE FANS IMPORTANT?

LIKED vs LOVED

We've ignored the inconvenient truth of marketing: our whole marketing careers we've been trying to get youth to like us when all along we've ignored the Fans who already loved us.

Seth Godin uses the analogy "getting elected" and this is what youth marketing used to be like. If you were selling mobile phones, you'd want the biggest possible market share. That's no different to getting 51% of the votes and winning the seat. Traditional marketing can't entertain the concept of focusing only on 10% of the electorate.

In the 21st century, youth marketing is no longer about getting elected. The guy with the most votes doesn't win. In 2011, Nokia began to report crumbling market shares around the world and financial analysts were quick to put the boot in, claiming that Nokia's real troubles had yet to filter through to the market. The company's most pivotal failure was not the decline of the brand but loss of Fans. In 2010, I wrote a paper entitled "Hey, Nokia, remember me?" citing the decline of Nokia's youth base. These were teenagers who were 3,4 or even 5 times Nokia owners. Core fans who grew up with the brand. How did Nokia react? It didn't. The company simply pointed to its market share (at the time Nokia was the clear global market leader). In response, Nokia was quick to rebuff the concern, pointing out record shipments and strong sales in emerging markets. They were right. By virtue of their own measurements, they were doing well. They were keeping the analysts happy. But, you know when 13 year olds start saying "Nokia? Meh…" in your research, you're witnessing long term brand decline. Maybe it's not filtering through to top line in the immediate future but soon those 13 year olds will be 16 and so on. Nokia has potentially another 10 years of problems feeding through the market.

Some of our most common failures in youth marketing lie in failing to distinguish between Liked and "Loved. Just because you *liked* the brand on Facebook doesn't mean you'll spend 2 months building something out of their products. What counts today is being *loved* - not by everybody but the 10% that count. If they *like* you, you might as well be invisible. Awareness means nothing. When was the last time you bought a Cadillac?

When we first conducted field research on the Liked versus Loved question for handset brands we found that 71% of youth Liked Nokia - the highest of all brands but when it came to Love, it came behind Apple, BlackBerry, Samsung and SonyEricsson. In fact, it is the Loved brands that have fared the best in the 2 years we have been running the research. Back in 2009, Apple and BlackBerry accounted for less than 9% of the market share but they comprised 22% of industry revenues and 62% of profits.

In business sense, *love* really does make sense. When fans love you, your marketing dollars go a lot further. You get recommended to others. Your churn rate is lower and you are far more likely to have receptive users when you launch new products.

Traditional marketing is geared towards making customers to Like a brand. Youth marketing means getting people to Love the brand and that requires a whole new mindset.

AWARENESS MEANS NOTHING

American actor Bill Cosby once wrote, "I don't know the key to success, but the key to failure is trying to please everybody."

When Coke, Nike and McDonald's invested in excess of $150m with their sponsorships and advertising for the 2010 soccer World Cup in South Africa, they wanted to please everyone - particularly Africa's young emerging consumer. Yet, how was it that 2 months after the tournament, the most respected brand in South Africa, as voted for by youth, wasn't any of these high visibility icons but the humble BlackBerry phone?

Cosby's quote is as relevant to the personal world as it is to business success today. In the era of McBusiness, the aim was to please an electorate. He who secured 51% of the vote won the marketing game. That's why we hired agencies to win mindshare, market share and buy media visibility. 51% meant winning awards, Cannes Lions and column inches. We measured awareness and constantly challenged agencies on how we could improve it. We all wanted to be Coke, McDonald's and Nike.

The awareness game worked when shelf-space was limited. You walked into the a record store and you chose between the Beatles or the Stones. Today, however, many products don't need us to walk into any store to be purchased. We listen to Spotify, buy on Amazon or watch YouTube to help shape our musical interests. Music may be an extreme but it leads the way in highlighting the challenges faced by all marketers: the game is changing. 10 years ago who'd have thought that you could access any movie or book at the touch of a button?

Faced with overwhelming choice we turn to trusted sources. Armed with the tools to share and recommend products, we're listening to friends as opposed to authoritative DJs, magazines and TV anchors. 65% of young people bought their mobile phones based on what their friends said not what the ad agency said. When I was a kid going to the movies, I watched what was the blockbuster of that summer. Everyone watched Star Wars, Indiana Jones and ET because everyone watched them. Now, however, companies like Netflix make the majority of their profits not from the modern equivalent of these blockbusters but through their back-catalogue - titles you can no longer see at the movie theater.

Take a look at how young girls are using BlackBerry phones to understand why winning the game isn't about being Liked anymore but about being Loved. The heaviest users of BlackBerries are 20 something females, often non-white. Girls aren't buying the cooler brands of Nike or Apple but "dad's phone." Dad is an executive who has power, influence and respect - everything they don't have. They see the phone as a symbol of recognition and belonging; a symbol of the establishment where they want to arrive.

Young people today don't recommend the stuff they *like*. 100,000 Facebook *likes* mean nothing. When there is no cost associated with "liking" a page on Facebook, the act of "liking" a becomes meaningless. Recommendation, however, carries an associated risk; what if it's a dog? What if your recommendation backfires and you lose respect? Back in my day, you were safe because there was only 1 choice. You either liked Star Wars or you didn't. Now, however, you have to recommend among thousands of titles. Youth will only recommend something they have emotional investment in - like a game they've spent 1,000 hours building the Taj Mahal in or a handset with BBM carrying 100 PIN numbers of friends.

Being Liked helps you survive, but think of it more as treading water against the current than swimming upstream. Everyone Liked Nokia and Nokia struggles to keep afloat. Being Liked works as long as nobody else is Loved. When Apple entered the market, it leveraged its Beachhead of Fans from the iPod and Mac, Nokia's market share rapidly declined.

The challenge facing BlackBerry and Nokia is one of culture not strategy. On the one hand, BlackBerry is a brand in the right place and the right time finding itself organizationally ill-equipped to deal with a Fan base whose interpretation of the brand story is very different from the officially sanctioned narrative. On the other, we find Nokia - a brand that wants to play Apple at its own game and win over the early adopters but will end up ignoring its existing Fan base. In both cases, companies are trapped by McBusiness 101 and the old school of "brand management." Encouraged and cajoled by agency big ideas and silver bullets that will relieve them of failing market share, they can accept only the one officially sanctioned version of the brand story.

You spent whole marketing career getting people trying to like you when all along you ignore the inconvenient truth of the fans who already love you.

FANS (NOT AD AGENCIES) NOW DETERMINE YOUR CONTEXT

On the 4th December 2011, a thread was submitted to community site Reddit.com with the title "The Terminator of Phones" detailing how the Nokia 3310 (now long defunct in most markets) could only be destroyed by the fires of Mount Doom. While Reddit is often used to excoriate public figures, the Nokia 3310 received a surprisingly positive response. 3 weeks later, a remix of the thread began to explore the seemingly indestructible nature of this phone. Redditor Naysar illustrated how an iPhone dropped to the floor "breaks the screen" while a 3310 dropped to the floor "breaks the floor."

Numerous memes followed. The 3310 cast as the death star in Star Wars, the 3310 as the hardest known substance to man and the inevitable comparison between the 3310 and Chuck Norris. The comparison with Norris is particularly poignant because they both share similar characteristics. Chuck Norris is a relatively obscure movie star. Most people know of him but few could name any of the movies he's starred in. Most don't know whether he's actually dead or alive (I had to Google it myself!) Yet, despite his obscurity, he's authentic. He's real but comes with a blank slate allowing numerous Fan remixes of the meme focusing on his apparent indestructibility. Contrast this with Bruce Lee who co-starred with Norris and was certainly the more commercially successful and widely known of the two. Unlike Norris, Bruce Lee's story is a done deal. We know too much, leaving no space for Fans to write their own version of the story.

When Nokia markets its Lumia line of handsets, it tries to own the official story of the brand yet fails to accept its authenticity. Official brand stories went out in 1989 with the Berlin Wall, MTV and Pepsi. What exists now is a plethora of parallel narratives told by Fans the world over. It's these stories, not that of some clever ad agency that will win a Golden Lion at Cannes, that Nokia needs to curate. If Fans love the Nokia for being indestructible and reliable then Nokia needs to build on this heritage. Being reliable may be rather uncool for Nokia in its egoic quest to overturn Apple but it certainly has helped Toyota build the most profitable auto brand in the world. You don't buy a Toyota if you want luxury or sports (although you may opt for a Toyota owned Lexus). The problem is that Nokia's looking at BMW and Mercedes and trying to compete with them on the luxury stakes. It's a game they simply can't win.

Many brands will spend a lifetime and fail at earning a moniker such as being "The Terminator" or "indestructible" or even "reliable", so when you get it you have to fight tooth and nail to retain it, not throw it away in search of something that will win you an award for clever marketing.

Build on the Context curated by the Fans. Leave them enough space to write their own stories.

LEGO FANS: THE POWER OF FANS

Browsing through the Lego offerings on Amazon you'd be surprised to learn there are a growing number of technical sets retailing at the $1,000 and up mark.

Exhibit A: LEGO 10179 - ULTIMATE COLLECTOR'S MILLENNIUM FALCON retailing at $2,200 and its 5,000 pieces weighing in at combined 23 pounds (10 kg).

Now, either there are a similar growing number of spoiled yet technically adept children or Lego realizes that the idea their bricks are just for kids are four walls they need to break out of.

Like many of the soda brands, Lego's strength has come from its product weakness. If you're retailing plastic bricks or flavored fizzy water you can't rely on design thinking or product features to sell or create barriers to entry. You are forced from day one to develop a compelling story - Context - to market the product. Being acute to the needs of stories have made these brands sensitive to the needs of customers. If there are adults equally passionate about Lego as their children then these Context-focused brands are quick to react and adapt.

Every time grandma buys Lego for her grandchildren or adult enthusiasts buy a Millennium Falcon investing their hard earned wages in another pack of bricks they are forced to answer the question - "why Lego" when there are equally capable alternative bricks available at half the price? And, for some, Lego doesn't merit the 100% price premium but for many, like Kevin Walter, it's what these bricks can do for their social life that he's really buying into.

Kevin Walter, a self-proclaimed hobbyist who ran numerous Lego communities and meetups online, is an unknown in mainstream media but to the informed, he's the guy that build a 2.5 meter high replica of Sauron's fortress Barad-Dur from Lord of the Rings. The entire project lasted 2 months and consumed 50,000 bricks. But, Kevin didn't do it alone - he shared the project online through his blog and sourced multiple suggestions, ideas and hints in shaping the build. Barad-Dur became the star attraction at Lego conventions, with teens and dads alike posing in front of the impressive structure for a snapshot. Cheap Chinese imitations couldn't do this for Kevin.

Lego's history of experimentation with Fans is long and not necessarily smooth. There have been numerous failures but there have been as many successes that have created emotional barriers to exit that prevent the Walters of this world deserting Denmark for China. Cussoo, Lego's fan submission website invites enthusiasts to submit ideas on what Lego sets the brand should commission next. Typical entries focus on existing franchise such as Batman with the Lego Dark Knight series and most have bubbled under with several hundred or, if lucky, 1,000 votes of approval from the community. So, when a submission arrives on Lego's radar that garners 10,000 votes in just 48 hours, the Danish brick maker feels something special is happening. What idea, you ask, gained 10,000 votes in 48 hours? Lego Minecraft of course.

Fans go to work when your brand manager sleeps. Your brand lives and breathes in their conversations.

VS THE FANS: WIKIPEDIA

Justin Knapp of Indiana, USA, is a Wikipedia Fan. What separates Justin from mere mortals isn't the simple act of "Liking" Wikipedia on Facebook but a more serious labor of love. 29 year old Justin has made over 1 million edits on the site.

Wikipedia's entry for "Red Bull Trolley Grand Prix" denotes winners since the event's inception in 2003, with Wanganui Motors Transformers taking the last competed title. Useful information? Probably not to 99.99% of us, but to that 0.01% it is highly relevant. Now, Britannica may out-perform on the big ideas

- the Kings and Queens of England, Obama's biography, the architecture of a fruit fly wing or the statistical breakdown of weather patterns in the Pacific Rim since 1946 but then these are mere fractions of the searches that happen on an ongoing basis.

The top 10 searches on Google on September 13, 2011 are as follows:

1. Angola
2. Miss Universe 2011
3. Raiders
4. Broncos
5. Manny Ramirez
6. Denver Broncos
7. Oakland Raiders
8. Wes Welker
9. Patriots
10. Oprah Winfrey

All of these are largely unpredictable. Britannica could never cover enough bases to know what people are really interested in. Wind that clock back to August 1st 2011 (6 weeks earlier) and you'll see a completely different set arise:

1. Randy Moss
2. Gabrielle Giffords
3. DB Cooper
4. D.B. Cooper
5. NPC
6. Ashley Herbert
7. Gabby Giffords
8. Marisa Miller
9. Kings of Leon

10. CSpan

Britannica loses out because Wikipedia is driven not by Professionals but by Amateurs - people who love what they do. The etymology of the word "amateur" stems from the Latin "amator" or "lover". Professionals don't do it for the love because professionals do it to get paid. Professionals care about their reputations, their careers and their next step up the lad. Outside of their work, Professionals go home to their families, go on vacation and empty their email inbox on their return. Amateurs, however, are relentless. For every professional there are thousands, maybe millions, of young teen developers out there messing around with stuff in their bedrooms, on campuses and in malls. Out there there is someone who knows everything there is to know about the Cable-Satellite Public Affairs Network (CSpan) and she's probably just 13 years old.

When Professionals clock off for the evening, Amateurs are hard at work correcting mistakes, updating the complete list of Asian Pacific earthquakes to include Sendai Japan or sounding out subjects a small team of highly trained pros could never conceive as being relevant to the mass market. So why then do we hang on to the myth that innovation and marketing is the product of clever individuals and not clever markets? The answer is culture.

Facebook and Apple have embraced it. Google are embracing it by inviting young girls to their Googleplex for a day of coding and app hacking. Heard of the Google Droidettes yet? If you're looking for social proof, I think the brands Google, Apple and Facebook are as good as any as confirmation that the innovation and marketing game has changed irrevocably.

"I do all kinds of odd jobs for money, but my most recent forty hours a week was pizza delivery," Justin Knapp told the media in an interview in 2012.

Advertising makes pizza delivery drivers feel worthless because they aren't rich/successful/popular enough. Youth marketing turns pizza delivery drivers into celebrities.

EVERYONE HAS FANS: NOODLES

When we think of Fans we think of teenagers getting excited about Nikes and BlackBerries after seeing them promoted on hip hop videos. Hip hop has provided a useful line of influence to brands over the past decade - from promoting Courvoisier and Krystal spirits to Escalades. So, when underground rapper J20 in Africa starts propping Indomie instant noodles from Indonesia, you have to wonder if product placement has perhaps taken a step too far.

But this isn't product placement, J20's decision to eschew the benefits of Indomie's best selling noodle brand was purely a personal one - he liked the taste. "Tomorrow," raps J20 "is just 2 packets away." Comments on the YouTube video range from disbelief to a whole host of Indonesian supporters who seize the opportunity to reinforce their noodle's cultural superiority over wannabe rivals to more personal attacks on the less informed commenters who ask "is it Malaysian?"

Back home in Indonesia, Indomie continues to carve out its student base of fans. Rival Mie Sedap (literally "delicious noodle") vies for their attention claiming a better tasting noodle and deeper marketing pockets. When Indomie focused on building relationships with grassroots Fans in the student world, Mie Sedap aimed to capture retailer shelf space and high visibility celebrities like Titi Kamal posing in a provocative angel costume. Ask any Indonesian student which noodle brand they'd buy, the answer inevitably comes back "Indomie."

World over, student Fans gravitate towards simple noodle brands. In India, Nestle's Maggi nurtures a community of their own. With over 450,000 likes on Facebook, Fans like Devika Singh reveal their emotional attachment to the brand stating "i love maggi i eat every day." Like Indomie, Maggi and even Pot Noodle in the UK continues to grow its grassroots Fan base one customer at a time by focusing on creating simple products that allow fans to share their stories. In India, Maggi actively encourages its Fans to share recipes and connect with each other over these ideas. When Indonesian students were promoting the "internet" in the 90s they weren't talking about TCPIP based gadgets but Indomie + Kornet (kornet in Indonesian is corned/bully beef).

If your product manager ever says "yes, but our product simply isn't cool like the iPad or Nike" then encourage them to take a good look at a packet of noodles for inspiration. This isn't about the product, it's about the story. Every brand has Fans, even yours. Their story is your brand's story.

If it's possible to get passionate about a packet of noodles, Fans can get passionate about your product too.

WHO ARE THEY?

FAUX-FANS

Mobile operator QTel from Qatar, like most of its peers, has its own Facebook fan page. It's a "fan" page rather than a "Fan" page because, as we'll discover that creating Fans doesn't start with social media.

Creating Fans starts with breaking down the walls that prevent being part of the company and the brand. In many ways, social media can break down the walls but simply having a fan page or Twitter account isn't enough - it's about the people behind these accounts that make it work. Of course, this is hard work. It was simply easier for QTel to hire a social media agency and outsource the problem to someone else.

The QTel page has over 10,000 Likes but when it comes down to dialogue, it's non existent. QTel uses the page to solicit contrived conversations with these faux-Fans. The term "fan page" is itself misleading - these aren't Fans just people who clicked the Like button. Posting "This week I'm most excited about _____" was expected to create a conversation with these Likers but none replied. People aren't interested in what your brand has to say, even if they "liked" your fan page. Rather than conversations about what you're excited about this week, customers used it as an opportunity to address issues about QTel. One poster, Gary Wright, wrote:

"I found it necessary to mention this here: one of qtel managers was blocking the way on the parking area of the building where qtel office is located... when asked to open the road and allow other people to reach their offices his response was 'I don't care let them fly over my car.'"

I doubt most of these Likers were real people anyway. I know a guy who'll get you 2,000 fans for your Facebook page for just $5. At 0.25 cents a Fan, your social media agency may think they're onto a winner here but bear this in mind: it's easy come easy go. $1 wins you 400 "fans" on Facebook. For a real Fan, however, the cost is considerably higher - 1 million edits, 70000 lego pieces or 10,000 hours on Minecraft.

The benefit of 10,000 Likers on Facebook is instantly wiped out by the negative impact one employee can wreak on your brand. But it's not that employee's fault for double parking the car, it's the culture that propagates an attitude of arrogance based on fear. When your brand is fearful of its customers, employees hide behind big brand imagery, brand stories and creative agencies. In real life, they're nice people. But once inside the world of the brand, they build walls.

You can't fake this stuff.

Facebook fans aren't Fans. Real Fans love what you do for them. To do stuff for them you have to first break down the walls that prevent your people from acting naturally.

FANS vs EARLY ADOPTERS: TREVOR MORAN

"I'm so amped I could stay here for 3 weeks," says a white iPod wearing hipster in the line that snakes outside the Apple store, San Francisco.

"If it looks the same, how will people know I upgraded?" shrugs another beanie wearing student outside the Apple store in Chicago.

The video runs through the pantheon of Apple fanboy stereotypes, mocking their public devotion to the brand before cutting to the curious coveting looks of Macbook holding hipsters glancing at a girl sitting on a bench playing with her new Samsung.

"Hey bro! Can we see your phone?"

"Check out the screen, this thing is huge," says another as a Samsung toting youth oblivious to the Apple store line up hails down a taxi, getting on with his life.

"I could never get a Samsung," dismisses the hipster staring into his Macbook, to which his friend adds, "Dude, you're a Barista."

Samsung's full frontal attack on Apple was met with roars of laughter by the mobile industry when it aired at the Mobile World Congress in Barcelona. How fickle and vain the Apple fanboys were. How grounded and authentic their Samsung counterparts.

The "Next Big Thing Samsung vs Apple" videos on YouTube reveal a key weakness in how technology companies see their Fans. For Samsung, Apple Fans are hipsters who hang outside the store, whose life has little meaning apart from conversations around product launches and a seemingly religious devotion to the Apple brand. Samsung calls them iSheep and it's a traditional, and very broken, view of who Fans really are.

Sure, teens and hipsters line up outside Apple stores craving new products but these, contrary to Samsung's worldview, aren't Fans. Fans aren't early adopters. *Fans aren't led by brand narratives.* Fans are very much their own people who take form a brand what they can and use it to supplement their own story.

13 year old Trevor Moran is one such Fan. On the internet, he goes by the name "iTrevor." He'd be, in the Samsung vernacular, an iSheep because Trevor hangs out at Apple stores. Yet, this is where the world views diverge. Trevor wants to make it in the movies - not necessarily as an actor but in movie production. He takes a handheld camera and a webcam with him to the Apple stores and records 5 minute sketches while he dances to a selection of tunes from Lady Gaga to the Black Eyed Peas. Staff and customers alike stand by in amazement. Most ignore him. Some join in with his dance. Officious staff from a previous generation force him to turn the music down or off. Either way, the show goes on and Trevor gets his recording.

At home, Trevor works on Final Cut Express to produce 5 minute movies uploaded to YouTube, the most popular of which garner over a million views. In those he is not dancing, Trevor shares views on editing, audio and graphical software to his 62,000 followers. The popularity of his format has encouraged many imitators to try their own hand at Apple Store dances. But, while they may innovate and change the format, it's Trevor Moran who set the standard and influenced a generation of teens to think about Apple products.

On the YouTube comment stream under Samsung's video a commenter adds "My Epic 4G Touch has a 60% bigger screen, bigger battery, faster processor, twice as much RAM, and 4G... yet is thinner and lighter than an iPhone 4S. So it must be crap right?" For Samsung, a minor victory is scored but in the war for hearts and minds of the change agents, they are losing. They are losing because *people don't buy stuff, they buy what stuff does for them*. Trevor Moran doesn't buy Apple because he loves Apple, he loves what Apple does for him. Apple gives him a platform to achieve his dream of making it in the movies.

Nobody really cares about having a 60% bigger screen than the next guy - these are merely logical justifications for emotional purchase decisions. But, when tech companies go after the Fans they only see early adopters who line up outside stores and discuss product features.

Content is what you make for them. Context is what you mean to them. When engaging Fans, make sure you know which one wins hearts and minds.

FANS: TRUE BRAND CUSTODIANS

When red-haired, overweight Roland Bunce aced the voting to outrank allcomers as the leading candidate for UK fashion chain Next's "Next Model" competition, we were reminded of McBusiness's fractious relationship with the customer.

The customer is always right, except for when he's wrong.

Next soon pulled Bunce from the competition citing irregularities in the voting patterns.

So how do you involve Fans? Companies have known for some time that they need to include customers in the equation and the results have varied considerably - from brand vandalism to creating passionate grassroots movements. The divisive factor isn't the recognition of customers as part of the process but how they are involved. McBusiness only knows the "end consumer" and involving them in the storytelling will be a case of choosing between sanctioned alternatives. When movie studios solicit the responses of theatregoers they're not asking them to change the story but simply choose between alternative endings. True democracy it isn't.

American Apparel is long renowned for employing skinny teens in its advertising. Like Next the brand decided it needed to involve a little customer love to help it capture the euphemistically termed "plus sized" market. The competition vote ran away with a leading contender - a plus sized woman wearing undergarments who posed in a swimming pool gorging on chicken or dripping chocolate on herself. Her unorthodox approach to modeling caught the brand's agency by surprise. After consultation, AA decided to snub the public's choice deeming it "not in the spirit of the competition."

If you create a competition and invite young people to play, you'd better be prepared to relinquish any ideas of what the "spirit" of that competition is. Just who, exactly, owns this brand anyway?

Struggling Nokia opened up its iconic ringtone to the creative community via a competition to seek the best remix. It would be Nokia theme but with a snappier backbeat. The leading contender by a factor of 4:1 was a voice recording that sounded like a cat being strangled while singing the Nokia tune. Nokia, in true Pop

Idol style, changed the rule and reminded us that this wouldn't be democratic and the final choice would be made by the judges. Needless to say, strangled cat never stood a chance.

Here's the problem: we understand that Fans drive marketing and can make or break our brand but we want to engage them on the wrong terms. We want the love and influence of the Fans but we want to do it on our terms (our "spirit of competition"), and therein lies the problem. Fashion and Music aren't popularity contests but real world interactions between friends and likeminds. Most teens hate the popularity contests of the fashion parade that plays out in school yards. Most people hate popularity contests because there is only one winner. 99% of your customers don't want to be losers. When asked to compete on these terms they'll take the opportunity to stick one up on "the man."

In 1989, DC Comics released a sequel to its successful Dark Knight Batman series with a "Death in the Family" in which faithful accomplice Robin is pictured in the final scene trapped by The Joker and bound by explosives. Readers were asked to vote on the outcome. 5,343 wanted Robin to die a fiery death with only 5,271 voting to keep Robin alive. Most real Batman Fans didn't want Robin to die, they didn't even want to vote on the outcome but DC opened up the narrative with a half-measure of democracy that ultimately backfired. The publisher was inviting its customers to exercise power rather than determine the outcome and there is nothing more pleasing to your average teen boy than squashing bugs or using a magnifying glass to burn ants. Robin would return in later narratives.

A Burger King ad hoarding in Seattle displays a cone, chocolate pudding, cream Frappucino and a Burger King logo in sequence with the words "side, entree, drink" below the respective items.

Humorous. Clever. But, the audience had the last laugh stenciling in "diabetes" under the BK logo. McBusiness experiments with democracy simply compound its fear of customers. Customers game the system, screw everything up for the brand. The net result is further distrust and need for control.

Love is about letting go. You can't trust the whole market but you can trust the Fans. Fans love what the product does already and are the true brand custodians. Fans don't want Batman or Robin to die because they have invested too much emotionally into them. Fans will keep the Batman and Robin narrative going even after the publishers run out of ideas. Fans won't vandalize their own property and fans won't vandalize brands they care about. McBusiness marketing views the brand as the property of the company and invites the disgruntled to express their opinion, share their voice in this ongoing narrative.

Fans care about the brand; customers care about the price.

WHAT DO THEY WANT?

MONSTER ARMY: ASHTON'S STORY

"I live in a small town called Miles," says Ashton. "It's a farming community and there is only like, 800 people in the town."

Ashton is almost right. There are 762 people in Miles according to official records. Despite its minute size, Miles perhaps embodies the American dream. It was carved out from the earth with the toil of early settlers who pioneered the new lands in the late 19th Century. Families like the Wrights -Ashton's descendants - arrived here in 1889 to break in 640 acres of farming land. One hundred and twenty years later, little has changed.

While a new wave of settlers from south of the border have set up their own homesteads, Miles still remains predominantly a farming community with farming values. Being an 18 years old girl growing up in Miles, like in any town in today's global village, has its own unique challenges. Miles is "old." The average age of the town population is twice that of Ashton's, higher than national and state averages. Take a walk around the loosely collected stores that constitute the town center and you'll struggle to find a skatepark, night club or mall hangout.

Town highlights, according to its website, include the library, the county jail, the "Rumley Tractor" (a 909 Advanced Rumley tractor, which sits along U.S. Highway 67, weighs 24,470 pounds and has a maximum speed of 2½ miles per hour) and the rather curious

"Red Brick Road." When town sources tell you that Miles Texas is "named after Jonathan Miles (cattleman and railroad contractor) who had donated $5,000 to a fund for an extension of a railroad track" you begin to form a better picture of how growing up in this small town is going to be.

Welcome to Miles, Runnels County—the town you've probably never heard of. Which is unfortunate, because it is in towns like Miles where a new way of doing business is done. This isn't a story about Miles, however. It's a story about about Ashton and that is the essence of Brand Democracy. Brand Democracy found its roots in soda brands because the prevailing conditions in these environments were right. Starbucks grew out of a base in Seattle because of the social conditions we discussed earlier. Brand Democracy thrives in soda brands because soda brand marketers know all they're selling is fizzy water. They are the marketer's marketer because they had long ago give up on the ghost that their product was in any way meaningful. All meaning had to be created - either by marketers or the customers themselves. At first this was a limitation. Ultimately, it meant liberation.

In the Big Idea era of marketing, small towns didn't feature because the Pepsi Generation appealed to a whole generation whether in small towns of Texas or the vast sprawling low-rise suburbs of California. To the marketers it was one cohesive playing field won through a game of attrition better known as market share. As brands continue to ply their Big Idea models on the social media playing field opportunities open up for small innovators who can chip away at the disaffected mainstream through offering meaningful communities in which these outliers can belong. But, cynics argue, all very good if you're pushing $50m in sales and are still operating in the minor leagues - does this model work if you're turning over billions of dollars?

The answer, we'll discover, is yes. It works because the challenges of migrating from $millions to $billions are organizational.

When companies step up over time, the needs of the organization outgrow those of the customer. It becomes a game of Brand Management over Brand Democracy. But not all billion dollar companies are Brand Bureaucracies. Brand Democracy can work if the company stays firmly rooted in the needs of the community it curates and recognizes the paramount importance of the stories told by people like Ashton.

Ashton's story is not unique. We've all grown up in "small towns" defined by our young mentality, our sense of marginalization and striving to reach out to the global diaspora of youth that existed tantalizingly in skate magazines, fashion blogs, Hype Beast or hip hop videos. We've all experienced the yearning for the big city lights to the sheer joy of those first few days at college when we, released from the geographical constraints of our upbringing, discovered there were people out there just like us. We weren't so strange after all. Ashton Wright is the voice of a generation—a teenager seeking communion with the wider youth diaspora but trapped by the geographical choices of her parents. Ashton is a teenager that wants to belong, who wants to be significant.

Miles, Texas could be anywhere in the world. It could be the bustling back-streets of Harajuku Dori or the favelas of Sao Paulo. It is wherever young people are the disaffected. These are individuals who have yet to find their place in the world. These are individuals who are trying desperately to unravel the layers of childhood to find their role in society.

"I am the only one that rides in my town, so I have to ride by myself a lot. Rodeo is really big here, so a lot of people in my town think that racing dirt bikes is easy and stupid," says Ashton, perhaps unwittingly speaking for an entire generation of youth growing up both misunderstood and marginalized by their elders.

Ashton is your regular American college kid—18 years old with a healthy obsession for the outdoor life. Marketers see PowerPoint presentations that begin with stock photos of skateboarders in high-five poses and patronizing broad-brush statements about how youth love social media, games and self-expression. But what most marketers didn't know is that Ashton is a rising star in her own Universe. This isn't the known Universe of "ordinary" marketing to youth, typified by clever advertising campaigns, focus group "insights" and high-visibility sponsorship. This Universe is brought into being by a new generation of youth brands emerging from obscurity to the big time, from niche to dominating the mass, and from being an interesting intellectual diversion to a threat to the established order.

Hansen Natural Corp - owner of the Monster Energy drinks line - is no ordinary company. In fact, it's probably a brand you've never heard of. But this is a company that is more profitable per employee than Apple. The company is growing its earnings at 9% per annum, sales at 27% while keeping a debt-to-asset ratio of 0.1% (ie. all their cash is their own). All this, despite sitting in the middle of the deepest consumer economic recession this side of the War. Being ordinary, has never been the recipe behind this energy drink's success.

One reason you've probably never heard of Monster is because you're not 18 years old and you don't live in Miles, Texas. Not that Monster has any geographical presence there. It's just a place where one of their stories is being told. And here's the rub—this is a company that doesn't advertise. In fact, the deeper we dive into the world of Brand Democracy the more we'll find that when it comes to success and failure of youth brand, advertising plays but a cameo role.

The real pivot points aren't media choices, but choices in mindset. Hansen is no niche brand. With $1.3 billion in sales and a market cap of $7.8 billion you could consider it as a major player but it's not playing by the major league rules. For Hansen, the first rule they were going to break successfully was the rule of brand management: that your reputation residing in your corporate assets. The logo, the advertising, the PR and the website—meant very little to this generation. None of these assets create Context. If Hansen was going to redefine the market, it had to start redefining the rules by which success was defined. And where its competitors had invested billions in high-visibility mass marketing campaigns, Monster was going to convert its customers one at a time. Ashton is no "customer," she is a fan—a devoted paid up member of the Monster tribe known as the Monster Army. This 18 years old from Miles, Texas is a rising motocross star and, at the time of writing, is featured in the "November Soldier Spotlight" for Monster's burgeoning Army website. Army, in this instance, means army of fans—one million of them—all participating in a community that gives them all a respective voice.

Ashton's story is intriguing. Not only is she a relative unknown in the eyes of traditional marketers whose worldview is largely shaped by the "findings" of a focus group, but also she is an anomaly in the world of motocross—she is a girl.

"I think in some cases being a girl has its advantages over a guy. But guys can make a living at this sport; I think eventually it will get that way for the women too. Especially with awesome women riders we have out there today," she says.

Ashton is an awesome rider whose story is able to inspire and motivate a generation of would-be Ashtons. Her profile on Monster Army is testament to the site's ability to support this generation of wannabes. Without the Monster Army, members like Ashton and Macca would have one less tool to achieve significance and belonging. A brand is only as powerful as the social benefit its customers can derive from it and from the brand's platform. Nobody's espousing the benefits of Monster; they are broadcasting their own stories with Monster's help. Vipe Desai, ex-head of action sports for Monster Energy, said that the brand's core strength was built around the stories of individuals like Ashton and Macca rather than some creative agency fabricated narrative.

When a whole industry is built around broadcasting a Big Idea, having your creative work play second fiddle to the individual narratives of fans may be a slice of humble pie too big to swallow. But, it's this letting go of corporate ego and recognition of the critical importance of the community's fan stories as the real brand story that has enabled Monster to behave like "the little guy" even though it plays in the big league of soda billionaires.

You've spent your whole marketing career getting people to like you when you ignored the inconvenient truth of the fans who already loved you. I recently read a report entitled "Strategy for Facebook Wall posting" aimed at brands. You can also check Emarketer's case study on the "Snack Brand [that] Doubles Facebook 'Likes' Through Social Coupon." This isn't about being Liked anymore. If your customers like you, be afraid be very afraid. Ashton's relationship with Monster isn't about Liked.

"We never had customers" says Vipe, "we only had Fans".

Take a look at the mobile phone industry. We ran a survey back in 2010 to highlight this difference. Which brands did youth Like? Which brands did youth Love? While most young people in our survey (in US & UK) liked Nokia, most would recommend Apple. By 2011, these results bore out - Nokia may have been widely liked and known but nobody was buying it anymore. You see, being Liked is what we did back in 1989 with the Pepsi Generation when marketing was all about getting elected ie. getting 51% of the market share. Today, however, as Monster proves, it's very different. That's why Desai doesn't talk about his time at Monster and the fans there in the vernacular of a traditional marketer; when asked about the nature of their engagement, he doesn't refer to fans being "engaged" but uses the word "ferocious." Now, when was the last time Nokia used that word in their marketing?

"Regular Man, None of This Goofy Shit!" explains Monster Army rookie Macca of his style "As Long As It Makes the Boys Jaws Drop and the Girls Skirts Drop, I'm Styling It!"

Marcomms would cringe. Consumer insights managers would gloss over the data. This didn't fall into the "4 Ps"—or whatever they're called now—and the "social media strategy." Almost everybody would ignore the truth that for Macca at least, this flavored sugary beverage was a Social Tool. Everybody, that is, except you, because you know that the product's Content is secondary to the Context it creates. Almost everybody would have missed a trick because they were focused on the Content instead of the Context. Most marketers would focus on how to make this soda beverage cool, instead of how to connect people like Macca. And that's where so much youth marketing goes wrong. It becomes more about the brand and less about what young people do every day in their lives.

How can you help me belong?
How can you help me be significant?

If you can answer these questions—questions about the 2 key drivers of youth behavior—about your products and brand, then the fact you are a nondescript soda beverage, a cheese manufacturer or a businessman's phone become irrelevant to the fact that anything, with the right amount of young people and hacking, becomes a social tool in its own right. Applying Social Thinking in the real world means developing deep insights into the forces that shape their lives and supporting the stories people want to tell about themselves, rather than interrupting them with tales of celebrities and images that make them feel inadequate.

Monster made the conscious decision not to focus on celebrity. Rather than buy into well known athletes, they'd curate their own. As Desai puts it Monster Army became their own "seeding process" - an incubator that helped identify a new generation of athletes and wannabes. Rather than design a social network that revolved around the Monster brand a core composite of the Army was telling the fan's story and helping an elite group of those fans source sponsorship and recognition.

Real marketing is about understanding the lives of people like Ashton Wright. She is no focus group, no brand ambassador, intern or campus advocate engaged in a brand marketing program to boost her resume credits. She's just a regular teenager who wants to tell her story. She is a Fan.

When organizations are seduced by the Big Idea of the creative agency we drive a degree of separation between the marketing teams and Ashton. No longer are we creating a canvas for regular teenagers to find their own voice but now we're drowning them out with celebrity endorsements and official brand stories. Fortunately official brand stories don't find fertile soil at Monster because the brand story is as varied and malleable as the number of Monster Army recruits there are posting their own take on the world. "Glad to See More Beautiful Girls Out There Banging Bars, Loving It!" says Macca. But Macca's no ordinary groupie. He's a 17 year old skater from Maryborough Australia for whom "life is great" and time is spent "nailing those tricks."

Maryborough—a small town in the middle of nowhere in the middle of Australia. News travels fast and Monster isn't even advertising in Australia. When you entrust the marketing to the fans, it takes on its own life, its own momentum. When traditional campaigns run their course, when ad agencies go to sleep at night, fans in small towns from Maryborough Australia to Miles Texas are out there videoing kick-flips, tweaking their dirt-bikes, talking about their latest hangouts and sharing everything.

Why hire an agency to turn prospects into customers that like you when you can build an Army that's this ferocious?

Fans aren't buying your products, they're buying the promise of belonging and significance.

DOTHRAKI: THE IMPORTANCE OF SIGNALING COSTS

"jin ave sekke verven anni m'orvikoon"

or translated from Dothraki to English that means:
"this very violent father of mine with a whip"

The original Dothraki language was created by the "Language Creation Society" - a non profit based in Garden Grove California - when HBO commissioned the hit TV series "Game of Thrones" in 2011. Like most languages, Dothraki has consonants and vowels - 23 and 4 respectively. But, unlike most languages, the lexicon is rather limited - less than 10,000 words. That's because Dothraki enthusiasts are still making up the words as the language evolves. The original vocabulary delivered with the series had less than 2,000 words, the rest has evolved on blogs, wikis and fan groups who meet to converse in their adopted tongue.

More people watch The Game of Thrones online than they do on official HBO channels. There are currently 194 websites where you can watch every episode, many for free. Because the entry level into this world is so low, everyone and anyone can take part. That coworker you don't like, your teacher at school or even your Mom may be watching and talking about The Game of Thrones. All very well, but what if you were a "real Fan"? You'd need some barrier to demonstrate you are a genuine Fan and all these come-latelies are simply riding on your coattails.

In the animal kingdom, behavior scientists call it "signaling cost." The peacock's resplendent display of feathers serves little purpose except to attract a mate. The features are too cumbersome to help flight and they make the male easy to spot and easier still to catch. There is a distinct cost associated with growing this plumage but as long as the display is seen as attractive, the cost becomes a benefit.

If the peacock's plumage allowed better flight, made it more disguised or gave it attributes conducive to survival, it would no longer be a signaling cost. There has to be some kind of loss that Fans are willing to pay but customers not to demonstrate their dedication. It's this cut off point like the 13th mile in the marathon that separates those who just turned up on the day and those who've done their training. In Japan, auto enthusiasts modify their cars by titling the wheels so they run at improbable angles. Called "OniKyan" or "demon camber," modifiers tilt wheels such that they only run on one side of the rim, significantly reducing car performance, turning circles and safety. To the outsider, this visible display it looks stupid but to the insider, it's cool.

When somebody looks at a meme and says "that's dumb," you know the signaling cost is working. It's the 13th mile at work.

Because everyone can get on board The Game of Thrones, real Fans are prepared to make sacrifices that others wouldn't understand. Real Fans are prepared to learn a language that would serve no purpose in job interview or international trade, creating a tangible disadvantage to their own life but that disadvantage becomes a sign of commitment to other Fans.

Language is a popular signaling cost. Not only is language hard to learn, it's hard to fake. It's not cool for a white middle class dad to speak like a black urban hip hop artist. That means it's acceptable for his kids to use hip hop vernacular with their friends because it will always keep dad on the outside. We can say the same of teenagers and their mobile phone "txtspk." Adults use punctuation.

A key aspect of a meme's success is the 'in-joke'. From the outside looking in, we don't get it, we call it "stupid". But from the inside, learning Dothraki, compromising your car, mastering txtspk or growing the peacock feathers makes sense.

Making your brand easily accessible doesn't make it any more attractive. Fans want a learning curve that makes them more significant.

HOW DO WE GIVE IT TO THEM?

GANGNAM STYLE: OBSCURITY

Korean DJ PSY's "Gangnam Style" dance track released in 2012 was supposed to be little more than a satirical commentary. Wearing distinctive suits and shades, Psy appeared in his own video dancing his way through locations in Seoul's Gangnam district in an attempt to poke fun at the insincerity of Korea's own Beverly Hills, where the fashion conscious young sport fake tans and fake body parts.

Outside of Korea, few would have know about Gangnam if it wasn't for Psy's song. The YouTube video, at time of writing, has reached ~~300~~ 350 million views with commenters from all over the world talking about "getting my daily fix of Gangnam" or trying out the moves in their local bar with friends.

While the Gangnam meme has gone global, transcending its Korean roots, few of these recent fans know much more about Korea's own 90210 than its name in the song. Obscurity is the first law of meme reach. The more obscure the meme, the more latitude for change. In the Interest Economy, flexible memes allow Fans to take the content and make their own meaning out of it. Context is purely subjective to the audience who interpret the meme. There's a US Navy Gangnam video, a college band and Gangnam aerobics video now on YouTube amongst the 5,000 covers and 4,000 remixes. Social commentary on Seoul has little relevance outside of Korea but the dance itself can become a meme to help reinforce belonging.

Because Gangnam is obscure, it's easy to write the story enough to fit yourself into the details. In the US, a DJ like Skrillex although not mainstream is already staked out; we already know everything about him, his back catalogue and what he stands for. If Beyonce or Rihanna released Gangnam it would be a bigger commercial success because the PR machine would have already invested into its release but the song would already be a done-deal and offer little scope for listeners to create their own interpretations.

Fans don't want the done-deal; let people make their own context.

SCUMBAG STEVE: WHY YOU CAN'T OWN YOUR OWN MEME

When obscurity is compromised, the meme dies.

The infamous Blake Boston aka "Scumbag Steve" shot to fame on sites like Reddit and 4Chan when a friend posted pictures of him posing "gangsta style" in his living room. The internet got to work creating memes of the new "Scumbag Steve" detailing his flaky, untrustworthy nature.

"Don't worry bro, I'll pay you... next week"
"Hey bro, can I borrow... everything?"

Scumbag Steve became one of Reddit's most popular memes with nearly 500 variants posted onto its database. Commentators on

Reddit were quick to point out that Steve wasn't Blake, had little to do with the originator except the shared photo. But, not to be outdone by this new found fame, Blake Boston tried to capitalize on his new found infamy by launching his rap career and posting various internet letters advising others who found themselves the subject of a random internet meme to make hay while the internet's sun shone.

Boston went on to make a guest appearance at the meme convention ROFLCON in 2012 and fielded questions from the audience about his personal life, what he thought of the meme and his opinion on the cult of internet celebrity. Within days, the Scumbag Steve meme began to die. A few hardened followers decided to remix a new thread by posting memes featuring only Steve's trademark Gucci baseball cap and dropping the picture of Blake Boston altogether but the meme lost the characteristic that made it successful - obscurity.

Before Blake tried to capitalize on internet notoriety, Steve was a fictional character. Everyone knew someone like Steve from their student days. The unfinished nature of the story allowed every reader to write in their own details, create their own story. If Steve were a real person, it would be less an opportunity to craft a story and more an attack on an individual's character, a story that put you on the outside because you didn't know who Steve was.

You can't own the message. You merely curate it.

THE PEOPLE vs GEORGE LUCAS

Boba Fett is, by a long margin, the most widely coveted Star Wars action figure. If you found yourself the fortunate owner of an original model with working rocket launcher you could be in the possession of a collectible worth $16,000.

For most Star Wars fans, the mysterious character of Boba Fett who said little but implied much, the direction in the first three original movies needed little improvement. It's when George Lucas released the prequel trilogies and gave the bounty hunter an extended role that filled in the missing gaps such as what he actually spoke like, who he was, where he came from and so on that fans began to protest.

If people loved Boba Fett why not give them more Boba Fett? Lucas could never have envisioned the Fan community's outcry that followed the prequels.

"The People vs George Lucas" was one such creative manifestation of the outcry. This fan movie debuted at SXSW in Austin 2010 to much acclaim. The movie is dedicated not to George Lucas as the genesis of their passions but to the Star Wars trilogy itself. The movie is a collection of frustrations creatively vented on screen, frustrations of born of childhood dreams shattered and illusions dispelled by Lucas' later works.

The "People vs George Lucas" website reads:

"So, for those of you who feel betrayed, disappointed, infuriated or traumatized by George Lucas, there's finally a movie for you, the fascinating, excellent documentary The People vs. George Lucas, which not only details the crimes Lucas has committed against his fans, but goes much deeper, examining the Star Wars phenomenon, the man who created it, its fans and the very idea of culture itself."

It's almost as if the brand took on its own life that transcends the role of Lucas as the brand owner. If Fans didn't care, if this was simply a case of "like vs un-like" they wouldn't have gone to the extent of investing time, effort and money into the movie creation. As the directors themselves note on the website:

"For all its criticism, this film is a love letter to Lucas from fans desperate to forgive him despite what he's put them through, that I enjoyed immensely."

The Star Wars Fan community is an active one. The grassroots project "Star Wars Uncut" spawned from one fan's idea (Casey Pugh) to segment the movie into individual 15 second chunks which were then offered up to the community as an opportunity to recast the snippet in their own interpretation. In time 472 entries were cut and spliced together from lego, claymation and computer graphics remakes to full on directed scenes featuring amateur actors.

When a brand means something to somebody that brand needs to be careful about how it evolves its marketing message. Although Star Wars Fans have individual interpretations of the original movies they are all agreed that there isn't one correct narrative - it's their story. Star Wars simply gives them the opportunity to retell that narrative whether it's in claymation format of dressed as a stormtrooper on Tatooine.

An iconic brand lives in its Fans and marketers sometimes need to learn to simply stand back and let it happen. Sure, keep making tools but don't try to overwrite these conversations by developing a monolithic marketing message that removes their ability to create these interpretations.

We are dealing with Fans, people who love the brand already. We are dealing with emotions and identities. Perhaps you don't know who they are. Perhaps you are trying to monetize the customers before the interests of the Fans. Perhaps you see their input as meddlesome or obstructive. However you view it, these vocal Fans think themselves right.

Create the tools, stand back, let the magic happen.

FROM STAR WARS TO HARRY POTTER: INTERNET FANDOMS AND FAN-FICTION

Star Trek has long benefited from an active fandom. On Facebook, the series has 1.6 million Likes. There are 66,000 pieces of Fan Art submitted to Deviant Art with everything from gay remixes of the original 60s cult classics to detailed floor-plans of Klingon battleships that never made the director's cut.

Fans keep the genre alive but it's not necessarily the old-school fandoms that seem best geared towards the digital era. Compare, for example, Star Wars with Harry Potter. Star Wars has 6 million Likes on Facebook where Harry Potter has 37 million. The only fandom that comes close to Harry Potter is Twilight at 26 million. But we can't judge fandoms by Likes alone. It's too easy, too cheap a metric of real commitment. Anybody can simply "Like" a series and they quite often do, especially if they are familiar. What counts is what costs.

Look on Fanfiction.net and you'll find a whole underwold of subplots and unofficial narratives written by Fans hoping to take the official story in a different direction. Some titles cover issues not yet ready for the mainstream such as the Star Trek FF title

"How will Si Cwan react when he learns that Soleta is pregnant with Thoth's child?" while others allow Fans to indulge in plot lines that are too detailed or too niche to feature on the official shows e.g. "S'kebi of K'nar explains in a letter to her brother why she has suddenly disappeared. This story takes place hundreds of years before the books' setting, and is mostly about Xenexian culture (as I see it!)."

Yet, when it comes to Fan fiction, Harry Potters reigns supreme with over 600,000 titles produced, all unofficial. Each is a personal rendition of official events: "What if Lupin and Tonks hadn't died in the Battle of Hogwarts... but a couple of years after? What if they had a daughter? What if she was a werewolf?" Each picks up the narrative where the original books left off: "The future generation of students are at Hogwarts and causing havoc just like their parents. However these students are not only sending Hogwarts into a whirlwind of madness but turning each others lives upside down. Can they make it? "

Old school "brand management", the Loudspeaker, is challenged by Fan fiction. In this model, where brands are templated and protected, there can be only one narrative. If Fans produce their own work they see it as a violation of copyright and seek to close them down. When brands try to stifle the multiple narratives they also stifle the hopes and dreams of Fans. It's Fans who invest their heart and souls into these works. It's Fans who create social currency for others to interact with them. Each interaction carriers a ticket from the original series. Each reinforces the original's place in their hearts. They may be violating copyright in the strictest sense of the law's interpretation but the law needs to change. Without Fans, J.K.Rowling would be a poorer author. Fifty Shades of Grey was a FF spin off from Twilight. Without Fans, there would be no Twilight conventions. Without Fans, Robert

Pattinson would never have been voted "sexiest man on the planet" for the 4th year running.

Fandoms and Fan fictions teach us 2 facts about Fans and brands:

1) **What costs, counts:** If you want to measure the health of a brand you can't measure it through metrics that cost little - metrics like "Likes" and "Retweets". You have to measure a brand through the costlier commitments, the commitments that take time and personal investment to produce.

2) **Curate the Fan narratives:** If you want to leverage your Fans you have to stop managing your brand. "Brand Management" is like 1989 all over again. **Fans want the official narrative not as the end point but as a starting point for their own stories.** When the movie credits "The End" appear on the screen their own fantasies and subplots are just beginning.

Either foster the spirit of Fan community or you fight it with your lawyers.

A HOME FOR FANS

Type "www" into Google and the first result you get is Facebook.

Facebook's sheer dominance of our internet lives touches everything from the Arab Spring to teenage house parties. Facebook's relevance to a vast array of potential users and their lives is its ability to remain a simple platform that neither commits to particular worldviews nor interest areas.

Driven by old McBusiness metrics, Facebook also attracts brands.

Facebook fan pages appear to be the perfect answer to an awareness gap created by a fundamental shift in our media consumption habits. The eyeballs lost to print and TV are showing up on Facebook so it's here that brands will continue to ply their Big Ideas but in more sanitized "social media" formats. Every brand has one. Agencies measure "likes" as a moniker of brand success and, you guessed it, "top of mind."

Within this story a subplot that undermines the activities of most brands reaching out to their customers on Facebook: Facebook "likes" are meaningless. You see, if our social universe was visualized as the *house*, Facebook is the *kitchen*: functional, not necessarily a place to get comfortable in but always the best hangout spot for house parties. Yet, it's in the *bedroom* that the action happens. There are fewer family photos in the kitchen, often calendars and functional items like shopping lists and school notices. In the bedroom, teens gather personal posters and clippings to fashion their den, topped with a "keep out" sign on the door. When their friends come to visit, they go to the bedroom, play on the computer, sit and talk or generally keep out of the prying gaze of adults.

Brands are hanging out in the functional kitchen where the real relationships are forged in the bedroom. Facebook users are deleting "friends" and reducing their networks to reflect their real world interactions. We are constantly being presented with updated security and visibility options that are removing people from our activity stream so that we end up following fewer and fewer people. In the future, Facebook relationships will only reflect real life relationships, the distinctions between will become blurred.

And, as with any real world relationship, the options are limited. Our posts are a popularity contest to see if our network approves of our activity and photos. We share less about what we feel and more about what we've done and are doing. As Facebook grows it becomes increasingly neutral, increasingly sanitized and less effective as a tool to engage Fans. Facebook is about getting elected - saying the least to offend others. Most people will hide their passions or mute them for the sake of not offending their network. Surrounded by your friends from the office, school and your family, where do you go if you want to talk about Harry Potter, Triathlon or DC Comics? Which leaves a gap. Once again you are confined by the limits of geography.

It's the bedroom of options that represent the less discovered growth opportunities for business. Facebook groups or fan pages aren't conducive to discussion or connectivity. Real "fan pages" will exist on the outside.

Who knew that a relatively unknown BBC drama would garner such support on the internet?
But look at http://sherlockfandomrules.tumblr.com

Who knew that we'd find small snippets of our former teenage lives so fascinating?
But look at http://teenagerposts.tumblr.com/

Tumblr, Pinterest and Instagram are, to name a few, services that aim to connect fragmented diasporas of the Interest Economy through shared passions rather than profiles. As Facebook becomes more functional, these emotional services thrive. By decreasing the importance of profile and networking, people can interact more openly around their passions without fear of reprisal or public castigation. You can now see why Facebook spent $1 billion acquiring Instagram. Sure, Instagram has some interesting take on mobile apps that Facebook could learn from, but the knowledge that really made Facebook hungry was how the Interest Economy works.

In the Tumblr blog http://theburninghouse.com/ visitors are encouraged to share examples of the handful of items they'd grab from their house if it burned down. People take photos and accompany their items with a short list and minimal personal information. Useless information but an opportunity for those with shared passions to interact. Brands can't hijack the Interest Economy but they can help it. Rather than set up their own Tumblr Blog, K-Swiss shoes needs to be promoting real triathletes who have their own. Lego could promote the works of fans like Kevin Walter (Barad Dur) with a "fan a day" rather than try to create its own story and content.

Tumblr blogs for your employees? Release their inner passions. If you work at Red Bull, I'm sure you are passionate about some form of extreme sports. Rather than cajole these employees with veiled threats about "brand management", set them free. I wonder how many Lego employees would be equally passionate about building projects, space, construction and so on. Employees may just be a more authentic and tangible interpretation of the brand but it's the organization (and the creative agency) that prevents them from gaining their own voice. Realizing Facebook isn't the right place to build a Fan base may be the easiest option in the long run - the numbers will bear out. The hardest thing will be letting go of the brand story and the organization.

Engaging fans, marketing - these aren't strategies that can be solved in a McBusiness way by agencies - these are cultures, people and mindsets.

Rather than ask "how do we engage our fans on social media?" we need to be asking "how do we break down the walls that prevent fans from engaging us?"

WHEN FAN ENGAGEMENT GOES WRONG

Following a three week trolling campaign by Something Awful goons David "Arr" Thorpe and Jon "Fart" Hendren, the results were in: Pitbull was going to Alaska.

Hip hop artist Pitbull has long been associated with pimping his personality to every available PR opportunity but perhaps this was one gig that he hadn't bargained for.

A month earlier, WalMart announced it was giving "fans" the opportunity to see the celebrity in their local store, they only had to be the store with the most "likes" on Facebook. WalMart sells more CDs than any other retailer in the US and Pitbull, in 2012, was one of their most popular artists. It made sense. Or at least it would have made sense 20 years ago when these kind of promotions worked.

Now, however, anyone can "like" a Facebook page. It costs nothing. Back in 1992, you had to buy, write and send a postcard. You had to buy a ticket, a CD, or join a "fan club." It all cost time and money. Each promotion had a natural "Mile 13" that cut off the timewasters. Trolls didn't bother disrupting promotions because it took too much organization and forethought. If WalMart was promoting a "New Kids on the Block" album back in 1989, it would be relatively secure in the knowledge that of the

100,000 members in the postal fan club, 99% of them were genuine.

On the internet, however, there is no shelf space. It costs me nothing to "Like" a Facebook page. There is no deterrent, therefore, to a whole host of 4Chan trolls who decide to co-opt the voting process and turn it into a farce. When Pitbull announced he was *"...excited to find out which local Walmart store has the most new likes so I can share the experience of using Energy Sheets® with my fans"* he thought he'd be heading to New York or LA but the trolls had other ideas. They didn't care about Pitbull or WalMart, they simply wanted to stick one on the popularity contest. Yes, the same contest that they faced back in high school when picking the sports teams, best looking member of class or yearbook. It's the same contest but this time they have recourse to rewrite the outcome.

Rather than work out how to outsmart the trolls we need to question the logic of what we're trying to do. You will never outsmart the Interest Economy. If you're trying to outsmart it you're doing something wrong. Rethink.

If your ad agency is dumb enough to run a popularity contest like this or try to engage your brand in a "conversation" with the market beware. The market doesn't care about you. In fact, there are plenty of people who dislike you, possibly more so because you've been interrupting their conversations the last few weeks with your own Loudspeaker message about your competition. You have haters and your agency is walking you straight into a trap.

There are 2 potential outcomes here. The first is one where you "roll with it". Compare, for example, how Bear Grylls and Woody Harrelson came off when exposed to the "market." Both engaged the community website Reddit at different times with the popular AMA thread (Ask Me Anything). In this no-holds-barred open forum to the anonymous internet both were challenged with direct and personal questions. Did Bear Grylls really drink his own piss? Did Woody Harrelson really make that girl pregnant at high school. If, like Harrelson, you try to steer the conversation back to your own agenda you're going to get a hiding. If, like Grylls, you roll with it and engage these protractors you set yourself up to winning a whole bunch of new Fans.

The second outcome is, unfortunately, the most common - deny it. Nokia closed down its "open" ringtone remix competition. American Apparel changed the rules of its game when featuring plus sized models. Next decided that the public really didn't know best when it came to choosing the "Next Model." Brands that want the dialogue but on their own terms risk alienating everybody.

You could have won the opportunity to see Taylor Swift perform at your school (sponsored by Chegg and Papa Johns). All you had to do was be the school with the most votes. The winner? Harvey Mudd College, Claremont California. Except, it wasn't. The real "winner" was Horace Mann School for the Deaf and Hard of Hearing, so chosen and voted for by the internet thanks to a trolling campaign run by 4Chan but that decision was later overruled by the organizers. Even Swift, facing a PR backlash, said she would refuse to play at the school (to her credit she donated $10,000 to the school, but at a much later date).

If you're going to engage Fans then learn from the mistakes of those who did it the wrong way:

1) **Don't go looking for Fans, Fans come to you.** Simply look at how you can break down the walls that prevent Fans from engaging you. Looking for Fans means trolling the internet for those who have no interest in what you have to say.

2) **Don't make the mistake of using marketing tactics forged in an era when shelf-space was limited.** In the internet era, youth marketing has changed radically. What worked when you were a kid won't necessarily work today - especially those tactics that relied on a unique relationship between brand and Fan that no longer exists today.

DON'T TREAT FANS LIKE KIDS AT THE MUSEUM

How to involve Fans remains marketing's Achilles heel. In the McBusiness model, Fans are the antithesis of efficiency: Fans are nebulous and diverse, defying convention. That's when they become an issue when you try to control them by practicing brand management.

Ask your agency and you get the McBusiness model answer: use Fans to help tell the brand story which inevitably involves using Fan energy to create maximum awareness (the modern equivalent of "make me a viral video"). What Next discovered was that fashion, like marketing, is no longer a popularity contest; youth don't buy clothes based on what the most popular kids are wearing, they're buying what their friends are wearing.

Engaging customers through social media is tempting because it appears to be a quick fix for 2 key issues. On the one hand, the "engagement" thing that agencies don't really understand but tell clients is their key priority. On the other, "top of mind" which remains a legacy metric of the Loudspeaker era. The logic follows: by "engaging" customers on Facebook you raise brand awareness. To use agency vernacular, "we want to be involved in their conversations."

In 2012, Salford Arts museum in Manchester England made the local headlines for ejecting 2 teenage girls from the premises. You read the headlines and images of kids smoking in the museum toilets or breaking the exhibits comes to mind. But, no - these 2 girls were ejected because they came to the museum during their vacation time, *not dressed in school uniform*. The reason cited by a museum spokesperson was "safety!"

Museums today struggle to get teenagers through the door yet resort to an old-school Loudspeaker attitude of control - "we want you to come but only in uniform."

Museums embody many of the challenges facing marketing today: you go, you look, you don't touch. When museums tried to make themselves more relevant in the 80s and 90s they hired consultants to spend the public purse in trying to make their exhibits more interactive. "Interactive" inevitably means a button you push that lights up a display. Having young children, I'm forever amazed about how museums aren't geared for those it should be inspiring the most. A group of young children tear around the museum, play frantically with a steering wheel, press a green button and then run on to the next exhibit. The Science Museum in London's possibly only engaging exhibit is a real Formula 1 car. It's not a new car, probably some 5 or 6 years old by the looks of the design. My son would love to sit in the cockpit and drive it. But, no, there's a cordon around it. Not only that, there's a sign that says "no photos." If my son wants to learn about F1 cars he looks at YouTube. It's an incredible missed learning opportunity.

When you involve Fans you're making an implicit promise - a promise that you'll help tell their story so that's why you have to do it on *their* terms. The technology museum in Amsterdam actively encourages children to run around the building, climb on exhibits and play. Children aren't castigated for running by uniformed employees lurking in dark corners behind velvet ropes and they aren't told to be quiet. It's fun and children want to go back.

Brand Democracy shifts risk onto the market but also requires a change in mindset - of curation rather than control.

Doing it on their terms means ceding to Brand Democracy and this is core to what successful youth marketing does. Give Fans a voice.

AUTHORS

Graham Brown has spent his life living and working in both London and Tokyo. A psychology graduate, Graham has focused his career on understanding what influences consumer behavior. He has published 4 marketing books on Amazon including "The Mobile Youth" and "Youth Marketing 101".

As well as speaking at industry conferences on the subject of young consumers, Graham has appeared on CNBC, Sky News, CNN and BBC as well as in print with the FT, The Guardian, Wall Street Journal and The Sunday Times. Graham is also a panel judge for the Mobile Marketing Association and social media / youth board adviser to UNICEF.

Ghani Kunto has been involved in the world of youth marketing and education since 2007. He hosts a number of business talk shows in television and radio. Ghani has 4 published marketing books on Amazon. Ghani is part of the mobileYouth team and a Co-Founder of Youth Marketing Academy.

THE YOUTH MARKETING ACADEMY

Founded in 2010, the Youth Marketing Academy aims to be the internet's premier resource for those with a passion for youth marketing. We provide books, briefings and training for youth marketers from brands as diverse as Nike to organizations like the US government.

Check out our resources including the Youth Marketing Academy radio show featuring the authors of this book - Graham Brown and Ghani Kunto

http://www.YouthMarketingAcademy.com

www.ingramcontent.com/pod-product-compliance
Lightning Source LLC
Chambersburg PA
CBHW061515180526
45171CB00001B/191